Grandpa's HOPE

BETH ANN

AuthorHouse™
1663 Liberty Drive
Bloomington, IN 47403
www.authorhouse.com
Phone: 833-262-8899

This book is printed on acid-free paper.

ISBN: 978-1-6655-4061-2 (sc)
ISBN: 978-1-6655-4062-9 (hc)
ISBN: 978-1-6655-4075-9 (e)

Library of Congress Control Number: 2021920692

Print information available on the last page.

Published by AuthorHouse 10/20/2021

authorHOUSE®

To Brooklyn,
May tomorrow be more kind than today.

Guide to Parents:

This is not a book for children to read by themselves if your hope is that they better understand the race relations they come up against. Children need to talk about what they are experiencing. There are moments in our history that are difficult to comprehend. As a people, we are unable to change what has happened before, but we can change how we go forward. My sincere hope is that you can use this book as a tool to begin conversations to help your child better understand how we should be living in this world we share.

Read this book with your child. Discuss any words they do not understand and talk about what they mean. I have not hesitated to use 'big' words. If you want your child to develop a love of language, help them own the big words. Children are sponges, let them drink.

Get to know your child; talk about what goes on during their day at school, during their time on the playground, and after school. Talk about the good and the bad they experience. Ask how they feel about the things they might be exposed to on the television or the computer. Develop an atmosphere where they can speak their fears and feelings openly. Being able to voice their discomforts will help them heal and become catalysts for a better future. Most important, listen. As a parent, I have come to realize that I am not always able to fix what is wrong in my child's life, but the simple act of listening is freeing. Listen to them—help them release the tensions they hold.

We will thrive in this world if we embrace each other with love and accept the capabilities that each person possesses.

Cultivating respect and acceptance of people and cultures we do not understand will enable your child to grow and learn in new ways. Empower your child with knowledge, understanding, and a loving heart.

This is a story about Anna.

In many ways, Anna was just like you or me. Her parents looked forward to the day she was born. As she grew, they balanced keeping her safe with allowing her to explore and grow. They looked forward to her formal education as she entered school while, at the same time, worrying if others would keep her as safe as they did.

Anna's parents loved her very much. Her father had very dark skin and her mother had very light skin. Anna's skin was neither light nor dark but looked as if she had spent all day outside in the summer sun.

It was this skin, the color of melted chocolate, that was the cause of her misery.

1

Anna did not have
many friends, only
a few little girls
that lived down
the lane from her.
Many of the children
at school ignored her
as if she was invisible and
did not exist. Anna did not
mind that so much; it was
the children who teased
her that caused an ache
deep inside her. They treated
her this way because she looked
different than they did.

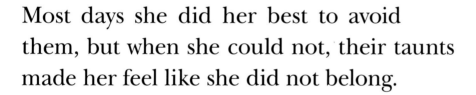

Most days she did her best to avoid
them, but when she could not, their taunts
made her feel like she did not belong.

She felt lonely and unloved.

One day their words cut her so badly that she said ugly things right back at them. This did not go well. Now they felt pain too and it caused their meanness to increase. Their taunts came more often and her feelings of not belonging grew into a reality. Each day it got worse, and each day Anna felt more and more alone. As she walked home from school, tears fell freely from her dark eyes.

Grampa was sitting on his front porch and saw her tears. He called her over to ask why she was so sad. She shared with him the misery she was feeling.

Grandpa took her hand in his and patted it gently. He said, "You have beautiful skin and when I look at your skin, I have hope. Let me tell you a story..."

Long ago, when the world first began, God showed his desire to have a relationship with his people. He rescued them from oppression and carried them safely through the desert. He provided them with water and bread. He gave them a structure of behavior so they would know how to live in peace among each other as well as maintain a relationship with him. Many times they strayed from him and many times he called them back. Finally, he could excuse them no more, so he scattered them across the lands.

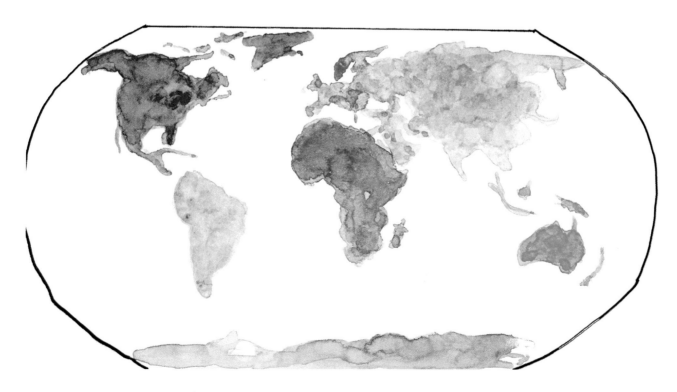

The Lord cast them out to other lands, scattering them one from another. Now the word 'scattered' is very interesting; it means to be so far apart, one from another, that they no longer recognize anyone around them. His people were placed on different continents, with mountains they could not climb over and with great bodies of water that they could not swim across separating them.

Even those on the same land were so far apart they were not able to see each other. Each was alone and separate from anyone else they ever knew.

They were as alone as you feel.

Much time passed, and these people evolved—each a bit different from the other.

Their skin color adapted to the weather conditions.

The people in hot sunny plces developed dark skin to protect them from the strong rays of the sun.

The people in cold harsh
weather conditions developed skin
that was more pale since it seldom saw
the light from the sun.

The changes they went through were not simply physical; the way they spoke developed differently. They each had different words that had similar meaning.

They also developed whatever skills they needed to survive.

Those near water learned how to fish,

those with flat land learned how to farm,

and those with hilly land learned how to raise animals.

They all experienced change.

The way they looked, the way they spoke, and the way they were able to provide food and water for themselves were not the only areas where they evolved. They also developed different ways of maintaining their relationship with God—their faith.

Different religions developed because those so far apart experienced very different events during their lifetime; yet,

God remained with each of them. He remained faithful to the promise he gave them, that he would never abandon them.

As populations grew and people began to move across the land, they began to come in contact with peoples from areas not like theirs; people who developed in a different way than they had developed.

Humans are a sad bunch. They became competitive and needed to feel superior to those not like them. They did not welcome each other. Instead of marveling at how each developed and why, they put up walls to keep others out.

This pains God greatly, but he trusts that someday we will realize it is a punishment to be so far from one another. There is great joy in a life lived together.

"When I look at your skin, I see a moment when two people marveled at their differences and reached across the divides where they were scattered. You give me hope that this world is slowly healing and reuniting as the people God made us to be."

With a hug and a smile, the little girl turned and walked toward home.

She knew Grandpa loved her and that helped her to feel better.

The next day...

Children's books tend to end with a "and they lived happily ever after," but this is not that kind of book. Our ending is yet unknown, but you can help determine if this will be a happy ending or a very, very sad ending. This is not Anna's story to finish, it is yours. How can you help Anna have a happy ending?

My hope is that your thoughts will contribute to Grandpa's Hope. Love one another, treat each other as you want to be treated, especially if they are not like you.

The next page is left blank for you to finish the story. What happens the next day when Anna returns to school? What can you do to make this ending a happy one?

I invite you to write the ending. Fill in the blank page and don't forget to draw a picture!

Questions for Discussion:

How do you act/feel when you are introduced to those who do not look or talk like you?

How do you act/feel when you come upon someone who has different religious beliefs than you?

How do you act/feel when you see someone bullying another? Do you join in to be part of the crowd, do you ignore it and walk away, or do you try to stop the bullying? How can this be done safely? (Keep in mind, children in a certain age group have developed sensitivities to not tattling on another.)

There might always be hatred in our world; but you can help stop the spread of hatred. It all depends on how you respond to the hurt in this world.

Index:

Page one: Our similarities—humans are 99.9% the same. See www.genome.gov

We all come from two lines of peoples which began in Africa; one line migrated into Europe, the other into Asia. See the Genographic Project at ibm.com

Page two: Talk about feelings. Have you ever experienced being taunted or teased? How did this make you feel?

Page three: Our reaction to being hurt could increase or decrease this pain. What are different ways we react to being hurt?

Page four: What is oppression? Oppression can be defined as when a person who is in power forces another to do something that only benefits the person in power. You do not need to go into great detail with your child, but answer any questions truthfully.

Page Six: Discuss evolution, the way humanity and the world they live in, change, as humans and the environment they live in adapt to each other. This is an ongoing process and is not yet complete.

Page Thirteen: Being competitive is not bad if we our comparing what we do today with what we did on a different day. Competition should always be against oneself. Each person is given gifts and it is important to try to develop those gifts. We do not need to compare ourselves with anyone else because each person has been given very different capabilities. When we use the abilities we have been given to feel superior or better than another person, it creates division between people. We do better when we share our gifts so all can benefit.

We do not always need walls to shut people out. What are other ways people might be shut out?

Overall: Discuss how we can benefit from knowing each other by things like exchanging what we grow or catch or raise. This is only one way we are blessed by living together. What might be others?

This book will help you gently guide your child through the racial tensions they will experience in the world today. As parents, we try to place children in areas where they will experience diversity, yet we fail to give them the tools they require to manage the turbulent waters they find themselves wading through. This book is that tool. It will aid you to help them to better understand what it feels like to be left out. It holds a simple explanation for why we have each been formed a bit differently. Finally, it will empower your child to be a positive contribution to the world around them. Each of us walk through this world filling in our 'blank page.' Help your child become aware of their page and better understand that it is in their control to fill it in.